WITHDRAWN

Pebble® Plus

A Visit to
The Library

Revised Edition

4D™

Download the Capstone 4D app for additional content.

4D See page 2 for directions.

by Blake A. Hoena

CAPSTONE PRESS
a capstone imprint

Download the Capstone 4D app!

- Ask an adult to search in the Apple App Store or Google Play for "Capstone 4D".
- Click Install (Android) or Get, then Install (Apple).
- Open the app.
- Scan any of the following spreads with this icon:

When you scan a spread, you'll find fun extra stuff to go with this book!
You can also find these things on the web at www.capstone4D.com
using the password: **library.08307**

Pebble Plus is published by Capstone Press,
1710 Roe Crest Drive, North Mankato, Minnesota 56003
www.mycapstone.com

Library of Congress Cataloging-in-Publication Data
is available on the Library of Congress website.

ISBN 978-1-5435-0830-7 (library binding)
ISBN 978-1-5435-0842-0 (paperback)
ISBN 978-1-5435-0870-3 (ebook pdf)

Editorial Credits
Sarah Bennett, designer; Tracy Cummins, media researcher;
Laura Manthe, production specialist

Photo Credits
Alamy: Randy Duchaine, 19; Capstone Press: Gary
Sundermeyer, Cover, 3, 7, 11, 15, 21; Getty Images: Blend Images,
17; iStockphoto: asiseeit, 5, kali9, 13; Shutterstock: amirage,
Design Element, Rob Marmion, 9

Note to Parents and Teachers

The A Visit to set supports national social studies standards
related to the production, distribution, and consumption of
goods and services. This book describes and illustrates a library.
The images support early readers in understanding the text.
The repetition of words and phrases helps early readers learn new
words. This book also introduces early readers to subject-specific
vocabulary words, which are defined in the Glossary section.
Early readers may need assistance to read some words and to
use the Table of Contents, Glossary, Read More, Internet Sites,
Critical Thinking Questions, and Index sections of the book.

Printed in the United States of America.
010767S18

Table of Contents

The Library

The library is a busy place to visit. Many people use the library every day.

The library is filled with shelves.

Each shelf holds many books.

Using the Library

Library visitors do research.

They use computers and books

to look for information.

Visitors sit quietly.

Some read books for fun.

Other visitors study.

Librarians

The library has many books
to read. Librarians help visitors
find the right book.

Librarians read picture books

during storytime.

Children and adults listen

to the story.

Checking Out

Visitors can check out, or

borrow, books for a few weeks.

A library clerk scans

the visitor's library card.

The library has many
other materials to check out.
Visitors borrow movies,
magazines, and audiobooks.

19

Learning

A library is a good place
to read and learn.

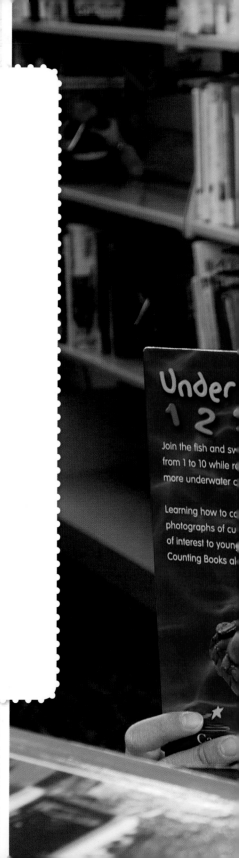

Under
1 2

Join the fish and sw
from 1 to 10 while r
more underwater c

Learning how to co
photographs of cu
of interest to youn
Counting Books al

Under the Sea

Under the Sea 1, 2, 3. Learn to count
~~~ut sea stars, octopuses, and

~~cially fun when you have colorful
~~ colorful foods, and other objects
~~Beginning readers can enjoy
~~a teacher or parent.

Titles in this series:

Baby Animals 1,2,3
A Counting Book of Animal Offspring

Eating Pairs
Counting Fruits and Vegetables by Twos

Under the Sea 1,2,3
Counting Ocean Life

3,2,1 Go!
A Transportation Countdown

ISBN 0-7368-1677-1

9 780736 816779

Capstone

Under the Sea 1, 2, 3

Knox

Under the Sea

Counting Ocean Life

1 2 3

by Barbara Knox

Glossary

library card—a card with a person's name and library number printed on it; people use library cards to borrow materials from the library; they promise to bring back the materials on time and in good shape

materials—the items at a library that people can read or check out; magazines, newspapers, videos, CDs, audiobooks, and books are library materials

research—to look for; library visitors look for book titles or certain subjects on computers

scan—to use a machine that passes a beam of light over the code on a library card

storytime—a time when children and adults gather to listen to a story read out loud

Read More

Clark, Rosalyn. *A Visit to the Library.* Places We Go. Minneapolis: Lerner Publications, 2018.

Miller, Shannon McClintock. *Find a Book!* North Mankato, Minn.: Cantata Learning, 2018.

Siemens, Jared. *Librarian.* People in My Neighborhood. New York: Smartbook Media Inc., 2018.

Internet Sites

Use FactHound to find Internet sites related to this book.

Visit *www.facthound.com*

Just type **9781543508307** and go.

 Check out projects, games and lots more at **www.capstonekids.com**

Critical Thinking Questions

1. What does a librarian do at the library?

2. Name some of the materials you can find at a library.

3. Describe what you like best about the library.

Index